Between Artists

Between Artists

NICOLAS GUAGNINI
JOHN KELSEY

A.R.T. Press

NICOLAS GUAGNINI in conversation with **JOHN KELSEY**

GUAGNINI: I knew what you were doing but did not know whether to like it or not. One day I went to the old Reena Spaulings gallery on Grand Street. I think it was in late '04 or early '05. There was a Claire Fontaine show. I became interested in one of the pieces, a coin with a retractable hook that could serve as a jimmy, and asked for the price. You showed me a checklist that had two or three prices scribbled next to each piece. I asked you whether the prices were fixed. You said no. From then on, I liked you. When, how, and why did you begin to like me?

KELSEY: Your series of "monkey shit" texts in *Time Out New York* was the first I heard of you. I thought I liked you later at Orchard gallery, where I sensed your mission was to bring out what was most nasty and contradictory there, and where you seemed to insist on the flimsiness and moldiness of everything that was then emerging (and already crumbling) on the Lower East Side. You were the only one smiling in the ruins of Orchard, and the only one who showed me his testicles.

GUAGNINI: Claire Fontaine is now more a brand than a con-spiratorial entity. You just fed it to Metro Pictures, a gallery that riffed ironically with the idea of branding four or five cycles of critique and legitimization ago. Because of my position of telling it like it is and attempting to ride on the contradictions at Orchard, I later became some kind of official interventionist. Kathy Halbreich recruited me to look into MoMA which led to the "9 Screens" exhibition. Once we had settled on the occupation of the bank of nine information screens by the ticket counter as a site for the show, I brought in Bernardette Corporation, one of your older brands on the market, and Union Gaucha Productions, one of mine. I am now so pan-icked at the salutary idea of intervention that I am taking a cue from a truly "unsexy" position, Martha Rosler's defense of realism in documentary photog-raphy, and I've been taking pictures of white upper-middle class mothers and daughters in situations of consumption. I'd rather be a photographer for a season or two than a sanctified anarchist.

My initial proposal for Orchard was for it to be a one year project. It turned out to be three because of the conditions of the lease, which was just about right as it almost entirely coincided in time with the sec-ond Bush administration. I was adamant about hav-ing the end of the project inscribed in its conception. Building ruins was a simple, and simplistic strategy to deal with instant absorption in a semi-dignified manner.

I have always been curious about how you handle

time and timing; you never kill your fictions, even when they dangerously take defined forms. I don't know if I like that because finitude is relaxing to me, but I envy how you squander your contestatory moral high ground by having this protracted and successful decay. How programmatic is that?

KELSEY: Your mother and daughter images capture the *jeune-fille* in the act of producing herself through consumption but also in the process of decomposing ("the *jeune-fille* does not age, she decomposes"). Piper Marshall and Alex Gartenfeld's apartment was an ideal "gallery" for their exhibition.

I'm not sure what to say about our particular decomposition or the rhythms of our fictions except that yes, I have always preferred the Dada self-terminating model to the Surrealist slow bloating and calcifying model. But I think that what allows Reena Spaulings Fine Art to last and not get too tired of itself is the fact that from the very beginning we've said we could always stop the gallery tomorrow. We always have one hand on the plug, and we are always stumbling over the cables. Then when we turn around and behave as an artist, there's a feeling of stopping the gallery every time. So rather than one final end we are always ending it and forgetting it. It's a sort of intermittence, turning the lights on and off and making a sort of signal that produces a consistency that's legible to at least a few people. But it's not at all programmatic; it's more parasitic in relation to the program of the art world and its non-sensical boom and bust rhythm. I think that, rather than ending on a note of prosperity and success in 2007, we wanted to extend our project into the bust, in order to see to what extent our project was merely an effect of the last boom.

GUAGNINI: Ah, the *jeune-fille* … In your prologue to your translation of Michele Bernstein's novel *All the King's Horses* you position her production in relationship to producing Reena Spaulings (she, not "it," in that situation), and pose a feminist(oid) question to the male authoritarianism of Situaitionism, and of Debord himself (which is somehow structurally analogous with Breton's affiliation with Stalinism and the calcification of Surrealism—avant-gardes with expulsion policies!). Theorizing a gallery in a prologue of a Semiotext(e) publication is a stylistic gesture proper of A.J. Raffles.

I associate the *jeune-fille* with Witold Gombrowicz's celebration of youth's immaturity, crucial to Argentine culture. But then there is the *Gossip Girl* element, which sounds more like boom and bust. Would you elaborate on the influence of Cecily von Ziegesar on your work?

KELSEY: Gossip, along with cynicism and opportunism, is one of the attributes by which Paolo Virno defines the post-Fordist multitude. Gossip or idle chatter … "a contagious and prolific discourse without any solid structure," describes the multitude's relation to language once the latter fully enters the place and time of work. It is always-already shared, and anonymous, requiring no external legitimization. Our work becomes chatty, and chat does not refer to anything much beyond itself ... it is the new productive medium, the production of communication by means of communication.

Gossip Girl's real protagonist never appears, she is the faceless source of this pervasive discourse, which in the book is based partly on telephone text messages constantly circulating among its various characters. Who is doing the writing? I guess it's a collaboration, a collectively authored "novel" inside the novel, or a novel written by its own readers. So *Reena Spaulings* took this as a model while attempting to elaborate a sort of post-literary novel, involving many authors, and branding this flimsy lit "BC." Another model was found in a book called *The Genius of the System*, a history of Hollywood's studio era. Here we learned something about the "stables" of writers that major studios employed in the industrial production of blockbuster screenplays. Many writers, each with their assigned task or specialty (comedy, love scenes, action, witty dialogue, etc.) working together, literally side by side with the typewriters lined up at a long table. *Reena Spaulings* also dealt with the *jeune-fille* (perhaps she first appears in Gombrowicz's *Ferdydurke*, as you say), a concept that allows a simultaneous engagement with Spectacle and bio-politics. The *jeune-fille* is a living, breathing, self-managing commodity. She is also an agent on the front lines of Spectacle, and locates her so-called freedom and health within its mechanisms, absorbing these inside herself and her language.

The series of *Enigmas* by the artist Reena Spaulings presented physical traces of the above. "Paintings" based on tablecloths taken from art world dinners, they are mute, but also made or painted with gossip. Unlike the recent abstract painting of some of our friends, these displayed another sort of abstraction: "real abstraction," or the story of life (language, sociability) going to work. These days, most work happens at the dinner table, so why not painting? "Painting beside itself"? Speaking of which, how did you end up painting with your balls?

GUAGNINI: Giorgio Agamben, so close to some of your causes, expands towards the biopolitical Foucault's notion of the apparatus, partitioning beings into two large groups: on the one hand living beings, and on the other apparati in which living beings are incessantly captured. In his distinction, it is not only the instances in which the connection with power is evident, such as in disciplines, juridical measures, schools, and so on; but also in ways less evident, where he highlights computers, cellular telephones, and moreover posits that language itself is an apparatus. Here he is also denouncing how the communicational techno-utopia is a post-Fordist quicksand where *Gossip Girl* can be produced as "communication by means of communication."

Nothing models, orientates, determines and intercepts the art historical discourse more than the perennial questioning around painting itself. Captured between the mandates of Gerhard Richter and Martin Kippenberger, of Benjamin Buchloh and

David Joselit, all semiotic and/or political models for meaning, including David's recent "network," must sooner or later be measured against the alleged historical possibilities or impossibilities of painting. So that's why painting, I needed to check that box!!! Whether we like it or not, it's our favorite apparatus. It *is* us. And it pays for dinner, too.

Testicling enabled me to enact and mock all the basic critical constructions around historization and the idea of genius, condensing the patriarchal and the indexical in a singe gesture. It was my most heartfelt attempt at male feminism (you plugged it for me in *Artforum* as a "brute, faux-macho gesture"). Remember that in his recent essay published in *October*,"Painting besides itself," Joselit makes the argument of the re-ownership of works and their meaning apropos Stephen Prina and Manet.

"77 Testicular Imprints" was also made into a book, where I pulled quotes and edited content of the publications that I had stamped with my balls. This created a quasi-essay made of fragments that read not unlike gossip. Curatorially, I could deal with Corbu and Picasso; Hitler, Stalin and Hiroshima; but also with Stanley Brouwn and Lettrism; with Ubu and Juan Downey; with Jonas Mekas and Paul Sharits; with Duchamp and Asher; and with the biggest swine, and greatest letter writer: Dan Flavin. Seventy seven, is a number that allows for a self-portrait through reference and a discourse complex enough to contain some metadiscourses. And then there was the actual pleasure of the making, of smearing my balls with oil paint and slowly or violently defacing the paper. It was cosmic and comic, seminal and scatological, meaning hanging between my cock and my ass. I loved the filth of doing it.

Anytime I fall into one of our classic rhetorical arguments with Dan Graham and he accuses me, and all of us, of being "neo sixties," I remind him I am, and some of us are, "neo fifties." I think the ideological genealogy of traces and gestures is operative in both my imprints and Reena's *Enigmas*: more Fontana and Klein than De Kooning and Pollock ....

Let's rewind a quarter century. When I was seventeen I encountered for the first time the literary experience of point of view and the voice of the writer being "universal" and "floating" while also being particularly modulated by and through each character and their debates. I am talking about Thomas Mann's *The Magic Mountain*. As an artist, I wanted back then to *be* that book. Not Mann, but his book. But I am too comedic and too sexual for that—I cheerfully failed. I am also confessing to something very unfashionable, such as Mann, while I should be advertising my fully-fledged Borgesian credentials. What were the literary experience, or experiences, that shaped you? Which texts captured your living being into an aesthetic apparatus and formed you?

KELSEY: At some point in grade school my class was asked to write letters to our favorite authors. I chose Franklin W. Dixon, the name on the cover of every *Hardy Boys* book. The reply I got from the publisher was that Dixon did not actually exist, that he was a pseudonym and that my favorite books were in fact written by committee or by corporate teams of writers. I felt partly cheated and partly fascinated by this revelation. My first "long book" was *Jaws*, which I bought because of the amazing cover with the monster shark rising up to eat the naked swimmer (this was before the movie came out). I also remember an encounter with the hippie feminist book *Our Bodies, Our Selves*, which I discovered in my older sister's bookshelf and smuggled to school in an empty Monopoly box to show my friends (that same day, another kid smuggled in his father's gun), but again, this was more about the pictures than the writing. Later, I was part of an institutional experiment where a few select "advanced" 4th graders were moved up to a 7th or 8th grade English class, which at the time felt like a punishment. Our first assignment was to write a book report. I had no sense of what a report on a book could be, all I knew was that it had to be around 5 pages long, and the book (I forget which) was over 100 pages. So I began transcribing it word for word in very small letters, then in desperation began dropping every other sentence, trying simply to shorten or condense the book through transcription, completely misunderstanding that a report had to somehow come from outside the book and outside the immediacy of reading. Anyway, my failed communication with Dixon was maybe the most formative and derailing of my early literary experiences.

GUAGNINI: It is ironic that your primal scene is the discovery that the author is a corporate concoction, a trauma acquired while catering to the requirements of an educational institution.

As much as you have experimented with the dissolution of authorship and attacked artmaking as an activity grounded in an expressive subject, for each of your endeavors there is a text signed by John Kelsey. *The Enigmas* series you mentioned before corresponds to "Dinner," your entry in *Texte Zur Kunst*'s critical lexicon published a couple of summers ago, and Reena is theorized in the prologue I referred to, and so on and so forth. You, the writer, are in charge of the official exegesis of you the producer of production. Your email address salutes Robert Walser, a figure as obscure as exquisite. I often feel that John Kelsey the writer is more a perverse and erudite prankster, an eighth grader, rather than a victim of an experiment for advanced fourth graders.

KELSEY: In the introduction to the Bernstein book, I was mainly attempting to contextualize the activity of my translation and explain how it functioned in relation to the operation of Reena Spaulings Fine Art. It was a question of mapping the connections between my own writing and the social situation within which it occurred. But it would be impossible for me as a writer to sign or take charge of all these years of group activity that in so many ways exceed and abandon my sad solo efforts on the laptop.

And here's how the *Enigmas* began, a story so banal you know it must be true: Reena Spaulings was in

London installing her debut show at Sutton Lane gallery, which happened to coincide with the Frieze fair in 2006 or 2007. We had prepared an exhibition of pointillist paintings of a slick condo high rise that had recently gone up near our gallery on Delancey Street (*Blue*, designed by Bernard Tschumi). A few nights before our London opening we're at a party for the Fischli & Weiss retrospective at the Tate Modern, and suddenly we get a phone call from Sutton Lane asking if we could provide a large horizontally formatted painting for their Frieze booth. The fair was opening the next day, so this was obviously an outrageous request. Do we pull work from our gallery show and drag it over to the fair, or leave the party and work all night on a new painting? Still on the phone with the dealer, I look down and see this long, black Tate tablecloth, realizing it's exactly what he's asking for. The next night we took another tablecloth from a dinner celebrating Christopher Wool's opening at Simon Lee and decided to work it into our Sutton Lane show. So the *Enigmas* began in London as the direct result of the contagious panic that drives dealers at fair time (all the time). But the "Dinner" text you refer to was more of an afterthought, nothing like an artist's signature, and nothing like taking charge of the meaning or reception of Reena's work. *The Enigmas* were made by whoever happened to be sitting around the table at the time (Glenn Brown, Lawrence Luhring, Christopher Wool ...), and by the dealer who needed to fill some wall space and inspired the idea in the first place. "Dinner" came later, and appeared elsewhere.

Maybe now is the time for you to explain "Power Structure," the group show you curated at Andrew Roth. Didn't you somehow place yourself at the center of this device? Isn't every group show a sort of panopticon controlled by the curator? What did it help you see in terms of your own relations with the artists you invited?

GUAGNINI: I don't think it is a matter of taking charge or of degrees of authorship. It's just that your writing reinscribes and somehow historicizes in real time these diffuse activities.

"Power Structure," also a reinscription, was similarly borne out of dealer pressure. I had done two successful projects with Andrew Roth. *Breakeven*, in which Gareth James and I asked that the gallery place a full-page blank advertisement in the 2006 summer issue of *Artforum*. We then invited seven artists: Alejandro Cesarco, Rodney Graham, Jutta Koether, Guillermo Kuitca, Seth Price, Nancy Spero, and Lawrence Weiner to intervene on the blank ad. The seven original works constituted a "deluxe edition." The balance of the print run of *Artforum* was considered the "popular edition." The profit from the sale of the "deluxe edition" was divided between the invited artists and the gallery. Gareth and I did not intervene directly on the blank page nor did we partake in any financial transaction. Then the following year I did *77 Testicular Imprints*. Both pieces sold. Andrew wanted another uber-gesture and I was in a bind to deliver. I had all these physical remainders of my incipient public acceptance: Buchloh's thank-you note on *October*'s stationary, Kathy's MoMA card, some handwritten invite to a collector's cocktail, etc. So I built a kind of Tatlinesque structure to paste them and display them, a "power structure," that looks like a crossover between a senior high school science project and neo-modern nostalgia. I then called a number of artists whose work I like and that are writers, curators, dealers, publishers, in short, that occupy more positions in the power structure than simply "artists." I included a '67 Dan Graham piece that proposes the replacement of art criticism for a three way dialogue among artists. Piper had the idea for "Middle Man," the three person show with Dan and John Miller (also included in the Roth show) which features my mother-daughter pictures, when she discovered Dan's piece in that setting. That work was directly juxtaposed with the *Between Artists* books that Alejandro edits, which is what we are doing right here. Reena produced a portrait of me so ugly I don't dare take it out of the closet more than once a year. Luis Camnitzer and Juan Downey were in the show. In the middle of the room, my structure functioned as a panopticon—as you described. The press release babbled something like, "Among the many vectors presented in this configuration of artists, the most discernable is a re-reading of the legacy of Conceptual Art. In turn, each share in the methods they utilize to disseminate their ideas: the public space of the magazine, video art, and the cultural conditions of production of several generations of South American artists living and working in New York City." It is as generic as it is true.

Yesterday I was browsing mags and saw your farewell ad to Claire Fontaine in *Artforum*. It contained the face of Karl Marx, four times. I envied the piece and wish I'd done it. Tell me about it.

KELSEY: To make a long story short ... Claire Fontaine is leaving us, moving over to Metro Pictures. There's no bad blood here because we helped them find this other gallery and negotiated the transition, agreeing it's the best thing for everyone, etc., but it always gets touchy when art world relationships change or end. It's also so painfully predictable, the way these things play out (the decisions that artists make). In this case, Reena wanted to publicly mark the moment (and all of its obvious and repressed meanings) with a sort of "ad." We always see galleries announcing the addition of new artists to their rosters, advertising expansion of programs, putting their power moves in our faces, etc. So we thought it would be amusing to announce a loss instead, to advertise a shrinkage, and—leaving the phrasing of the ad somewhat open—maybe even an inability or refusal to continue together. Those ads are pretty expensive, too, so it was a total waste of gallery cash announcing this loss (of an artist, of capital) ... a loss marked by a loss. The only copy in the ad is "CLAIRE FONTAINE IS NO LONGER WORKING HERE." This also refers to the "human strike" theme of their final show with us, and the ad coincided roughly with that show's closing, and also with the installation of a CF neon over the entrance to Elizabeth Dee's "Independent Fair" at the old DIA space in Chelsea (which in turn coincided with the Armory fair). So the ad is a temporal marker, marking a moment where a lot of different relationships were in some cases coming undone and in other cases solidifying under the pressure of the current recession. We were actually opposed to CF's contribution to the Independent because we knew it would only function as a logo there, like a free ad for the fair. But the artist really wanted the exposure, and used the situation to mark its own move over to Metro (their sign was "courtesy of" both Metro and RSFA).

There are so many tensions and contradictions in the co-dependent relationship between an artist and a dealer. The two functions co-produce each other. Reena Spaulings sometimes tries to make art out of this, and this has its therapeutic side. It was also therapeutic for us to paint portraits of all the other art dealers we've become associated with over the years (*The Dealers*, 2007). Relationships between dealers are always interesting, so many forced smiles, so much muscle flexing. This is one of the reasons we actually like doing art fairs, because it's the only time the dealers show up all together in the same space, on the same supermarket shelf, and we've learned a lot watching other dealers performing for each other there. Normally dealers stick to their own territory but the fair is like a dealer orgy (Mike Kelley once said that artists shouldn't go to fairs because it's like watching your parents have sex).

GUAGNINI: Was my portrait intended as a portrait of a dealer? I still own ten percent of Art Sales and Services

(ASS), the limited liability corporation that controlled Orchard. The last institutional sales are still trickling in. You know how long it takes to go through committees and boards .... How do you deal with sales? I mean with the very act, the tedious explanation of the work and its qualities to someone whom you might respect or not, the moment of the discount ... the miseries of commerce?

KELSEY: Your portrait was our first of a curator, and I'm sorry if it struck you as ugly. As for selling things, I have no problem with that. One of my main problems with artists is the pretense that their own tedium is somehow above or separate from the tedium of selling, a distinction that they continue to enforce in their gestures and time-worn habits ("the artist's life"). It's also my problem with critics and historians—the feigned neutrality of the discourse, going on as if their language were something pure and detached from business and life, and the more detached therefore the more critical. Artists though, they have a way of endlessly constructing formal freedoms around the normalization of the artist-dealer (and artist-critic) relationship, and they always get sad when this relationship is questioned. Artists can only continue being artists if they have dealers who continue relating to them as dealers, and critics sitting at a safe remove. For us it was never really about embracing business, it's about using the dealer role to say something about the artist role. It's playing against the efficiency of a certain division of labor. And I don't prefer artists to collectors. Some collectors I know are much more intelligent about art than some art historians I know, and much more interesting to talk to.

Orchard, from my perspective (three blocks away), seemed to fetishize institutional power ... universities and museums. There was always this need to have a PhD connected to a show or event, or an *October* connection, a vitrine, a seriousness. And now you have been moving behind the walls of MoMA, which seems a rather natural or easy transition, from Orchard to the museum. Do you ever feel like one of those animals in Kafka's writing?

GUAGNINI: If there is a Kafka story I identify with it's "In the Penal Colony," in which the written sentence is inflicted on the accused, who is ultimately sentenced without a trial, by a torture machine that inscribes it in his body, hence fulfilling the sentence. Again, I don't identify with the victim, the machine operator or Kafka, but with the narration itself.

It's strange ... you started differentiating me from the Orchard pretense, and come back at me with a demand on its general tone. I agree with your attack on the false pretenses of purity and disciplinary autonomy for art and criticism. Selling is part of the work, of course. Exchange value is everyday life. That's what "Power Structure" was about, curatorially. Art historians often work for dealers, besides working for and from Ivy League ivory towers. And many collectors understand things about art that people who don't own it do not understand and never will.

My own position: I took my strategic clues from Liberation Theology and Paulo Freire's *Pedagogy of the Oppressed*. You take on major blocks of disciplinary knowledge intersecting power (religion, education) and subvert them from the inside. So, yes, I am a full-fledged fetishist. Fetishism, insofar as it is a projective attempt to resolve the castration anxiety, is in this context synonymous with "institutional power."

We'll tackle the whole MoMA experience shortly—let's stay on the Lower East Side for a little longer.

I always felt, three blocks away from Reena myself, that the question of style associated with a contestatory halo functioned in your space in the same way that the *October/Grey Room* connection was operative in Orchard ... Reena Spaulings is the only gallery that ever made me question my haircut as I walked in; that's why I wore a Staples button stating, *Hablo Español* to one of your openings. I always find legitimating hyper-style somewhat refractory. Martin Kippenberger and Colin de Land are dead!

KELSEY: And Kippenberger and De Land are not the only corpses amongst us! I remember once at Orchard when Dan Graham said that the problem with Reena was that it was too "chic"! That was pretty funny. Orchard had a style too, a sort of yogurt and plywood thing, and smudged eyeglasses and carefully organized reading material sitting there, not to mention the styles of socializing and gossiping, and the way bodies (darkly clad) clustered as if in a *New Yorker* cartoon, etc. There is always style, in everything we do. I like how Deleuze thinks about style, especially when discussing writing and tennis. Style is how you get past yourself, the way to get around obstacles. I didn't mean to pin you down to Orchard or its style, I was actually more curious about how your particular way of moving works, how you move from there (out of there!) to MoMA and other sites. I remember that on the final, closing day of Orchard you had timed a solo show at Fruit & Flower—another, much different type of gallery a few blocks away. For that show you designed neckties.

GUAGNINI: Your stylistic description of Orchard as a *New Yorker* cartoon points to an important aspect of its aesthetics and ethos: it was a very Jewish gallery. Kind of the Upper West Side post-New Left bourgeoisie meets the Lower East Side. Reena, on the other hand, is Cologne redux, an iconographical and Catholic endeavor despite your own prototypical WASPness.

An aspect I would not like to overlook of Orchard's liberal humanist ethos, with all its self-deprecating guilt and its normalizing democratic assumptions, (on which I'll elaborate later when we discuss MoMA, which I choose to postpone again), was its political commitment, and my role in it. I am referring to the "September 11 1973" show I curated, and to the *SSS* piece in the bathroom by Jeff Preiss and yours truly, which featured a picture of Bush inside the toilet bowl, and which was briefly censored by the Belgium-state-sponsored-anarchist and conservative hippie Jef Geys, with the subservient acquiescence of R.H. Quaytman and Rhea Anastas' cheerleading. The refusal of the solo show was the center of a heated discussion within Orchard, and Sadie Benning's solo outing articulated the fallout between myself and most of the other members. On closing day, which conjured the full spectrum of our public legitimacy (Jerry Saltz and Roberta Smith, you and Emily Sundblad, all the Octoberized and Grey Roomed post-minimal artistic glories whom we exhibited and discussed and several of the art historians who also routinely discuss them, a specific art world wing of the LGBT community, and so on, and so forth, and so what), I opened a solo show in the now defunct first incarnation of the Fruit and Flower Deli. Rodrigo Mallea Lira, who runs that ghost "gallery," is a Chilean forcedly exiled to Sweden in his childhood, right after the '73 coup. So I bonded with him because we are both children of the failed revolution. I am attracted to experiments with the gallery form, such as Rodrigo's or Alex's and Piper's. I wanted to enact some kind of opportunistic procession of all these luminaries from one venue in the Lower East Side to another. I wore the tie I featured in that show to both the closing and the opening. You know I militantly dress down, so dressing up for the closing was a gesture not unlike your farewell ad to Claire Fontaine. The tie, that repeats the word "capitalism" in the typography and green color scheme used for the dollar bill, was a collaboration with a Harvard kid named Alexander Olch. He's incredibly hip, a filmmaker running a niche business of hand made silk ties sold at Bergdorf Goodman and Opening Ceremony. I wanted to check the "art-as-fashion" box too, and doing so as a goodbye gesture to Orchard, where I finished at odds with almost everyone, was to me a proper stylistic turn of the screw.

You affect a fake dressing down, with very specific subcultural and critical connotations. I am talking about your pseudo Navajo Ralph Lauren wool shirt. But what interests me more are your caps, which to me nuance your grimness to dimensions of meaning that are way beyond "punctum." Tell me about your caps and your political involvement with the Tarmac 9, the Invisible Committee, et al. They are certainly not going to Metro Pictures. You enacted some other type of procession in Union Square, not far from Seth Price's new loft.

KELSEY: Ralph Lauren—who's at least as Jewish as Orchard —is such a vague style, so generic (straight, gay, urban, suburban?) that I don't think it makes much of a statement at all, really, until you twist it a little this way or that. It works as a kind of a base-coat. Riding the hellish L train to Williamsburg, it's actu-ally rare not to be sharing a car with at least three doppelgangers. I'm conscious of being half-disap-peared and absorbed in a nasty monoculture here, but it takes too much energy to differentiate oneself. The cap just puts a cap on the disaster of being so whatever in New York. It's a capitulation.

We don't have to talk about MoMA if you'd prefer not to. Maybe you'd like to say something more about your testicular imprints? I'd actually like to hear about your feminism and how it's articulated via your balls, in that particular instance. I'm also curious about your castration complex. I really don't know much about psychoanalysis.

GUAGNINI: About my own castration complex all I would say is that my mother is a psychoanalist and a feminist. Feminism is naturally a default position anywhere left of Gagosian, and more so for us born in the sixties. So the question is not whether to subscribe to an ideological struggle but how can this be made whole with who I am. In the standard re-reading of essentialist feminism (Laura Cottingham), if femininity and masculinity are constructs, they are only partially so: men and women nonetheless have fundamental biological differences. I can only truly "speak" from my testicles, from my biological position in that struggle in which I am always-already an oppressor.

The book for "77 Testicular Imprints" opens with seven utterances: patriarchy, private property, power, progress, position, packaging, personality, which combined yield the formula for the perfectly "successful" artist, potentially constructing a genius. I also thought that in the master narrative of male genital art, AbEx, Acconci's masturbation, Mathew Barney's gymnastic saga of sexual differentiation, they all take themselves too seriously. But, I am serious about this piece being male feminism. This entails to laugh mainly at myself as a white Latin Jewish straight male, but also at a certain PC aspect of feminism as an academic and art world discourse. How's your feminism doing, by the way? Whilst the *jeune-fille,* as you claim, can be a figure of discourse where biopolitics and a critique of the spectacle intersect, she can also be immediately constructed as an objectifiable little slut—the basic commodity of the fashion-art-tv complex. Between, to, and from sexy to sexist there is a no man's land where the fashion police and the academic police are out there to get you—and her.

KELSEY: *Premiers matériaux pour une théorie de la jeune-fille* is a book by Tiqqun that came out in 2001. It calls itself "trash theory," as it is constructed around a series of citations lifted from the covers and content of mainstream women's and lifestyle magazines (*Cosmopolitan*, *Self*, etc.), pasting these into a discourse that references Foucault's late work on biopolitics and the care of the self. It is not at all an academic book, it comes from somewhere else. "The *jeune-fille* as technique of the self," "the *jeune-fille* as social relation," "the *jeune-fille* as living money," and "the *jeune-fille* as war machine" are some of its chapters. So, the theory is a critique of the *jeune-fille* that turns a certain advertising-type discourse back on itself, that attempts to understand the commodification of the self and the neo-liberal ideology of self-enterprise in relation to the biopolitical management of health, life and nothingness under Empire. "She" is not gender-specific, she includes all citizens of the metropolis, including men and old people. We are all *jeunes-filles*.

GUAGNINI: Then, what would be an outside to the *jeune-fille*? And what would be an outside to feminism within any contestatory discourse?

KELSEY: In the metropolis, the *jeune-fille* is inescapable. She is a surveillance camera, an ad, a yoga champion, a green consumer, a discourse, a medicine, a money, a depression, a fun. She is in your balls, too. She must go to war with herself, it's the only way.

GUAGNINI: I agree, we must be at war with ourselves. This aligns with my *spiel* on subverting disciplinary blocks of knowledge from the inside, and with your recognition of market conditions as part of our productive situation—consumption is production. But, I still cannot distill anything in relationship to gender here. Mapping difference of course is inevitably an apparatus. That's the curse of cultural studies. Bridge the gap between the *jeune-fille* and feminism, as you hint on the prologue to Bernstein's novel.

KELSEY: Two dudes challenging each other's feminism, this doesn't bode well. I think it's less a question of *what* is a woman or a feminist than how someone inhabits that predicate, or how we inhabit the gap that separates us both from our gender assignment and our declared Leftism. The *jeune-fille* is a sort of feminism that speaks back in the re-appropriated language of the very apparatus it wants to destroy: *Elle*. It works in the gap between *elle* and *elle*, *elle* and *nous*.

It is impossible to imagine a revolution that is not

feminist, but feminism needs to fight itself too, otherwise it risks confusing its potential radicality with matriarchal forms of control, which are no better than the "hard" patriarchal forms. Somewhere it has been suggested that networks are a matriarchal form.

GUAGNINI: In regards to "networks," a total buzzword at this point, we need a working definition and a taxonomy. The CIA can be described as a hierarchical network composed of several horizontal networks. This does not make it any better or establishes ontological differences for patriarchal and matriarchal oppression.

KELSEY: I'm not actually sure why a network would be matriarchal. Maybe this idea had something to do with the feeling of a motherly embrace, our general infantilism today, and the perceived softness of everything molecular. It does sound paranoiac. And it's not my idea so I won't push it. On the other hand, these boys clubs continue to claim territories in the art world. Isn't there a point where we all decide how much to allow ourselves to participate in and how far to identify with these convivial fraternities that always organize themselves in our midst, and which of course include women?

GUAGNINI: As much as I agree, and you well know that my primary collaborator for a decade was a woman, and in fact I always quality control my production against a woman I love, I have a boys club fantasy.

Curiously enough one of the writers that obsesses

me the most is Michel Houllebecq. Total male swine paranoia. I don't think it is even in fashion anymore to be for or against him—it's *passé*. But I have the desire that he write about my work from a paranoid perspective.

KELSEY: You and Richard Prince. But I suppose Houellebecq would rather stick to his own misery. It wouldn't be much of a club, I think, with him.

What do you mean about quality controlling against a woman? That sounds ... controlling. I'm not sure what to do with your swine feminism, Nic.

GUAGNINI: Of course it's all controlling. Isn't Houllebecq informed by both Sade's and Choderlos de Laclos's justifications of sexual intrigues and excesses, which are nothing but forms of control codified in literary forms? What I mean is that while I do not honestly think neither you nor I can really make a significant contribution to feminist theory or militancy, supporting a position implies living your life accordingly. In my case, this has manifested itself in a curious productive structure, which I cannot claim is particularly feminist in a socially useful manner, but that certainly implies a recognition of an equality at the deepest level. I am always in relationships with women artists whom I deeply admire and against whose criteria I am constantly negotiating mine. It's a position in my subjective and epistemic horizon that kind of defines me, even if I perpetually associate myself with male "masters," and master narratives not unlike the clubs you mentioned ...

you know: Roberto Jacoby, Dan Graham, Juan Downey, John Miller, Luis Camnitzer.

KELSEY: Houellebecq describes the impotence of the swine before the ever-glowing porno screen of post-'68 culture, the limp dick at the end of sexual liberation.

Maybe now would be the time to return to mommy MoMA and your recent work there. How was she?

GUAGNINI: Houellebecq also upholds some kind of return to a primitive and primitivist sexual economy, ironically in sync with Marx's and Engel's assumptions about communism being the original primitive economy. Influenced by Catholicism, Houellebecq makes all his male swine characters pay dearly once they access that lost primitive sexuality. For me he is the writer who has really absorbed Foucault and presented his knowledge as and in everyday life in a plausible narrative.

As for she-MoMA, foreplay was more exciting than intercourse. But I'd rather talk about our common experience with her. How did you feel about making art for a lobby, with a captive audience of thousands?

KELSEY: I like reading Houellebecq but I don't see much Foucault either in his primitivism or in this figure of the crucified white male who basically just follows the nihilist logic of an imploded society to its end. I heard that he's actually a Stalinist.

MoMA was like getting dipped in quicksand. The lobby is a lot like an airport terminal, and the video screens can only function like those in airports. We (Bernadette Corporation) didn't see it as a place to present video art. Instead, we tried to make an image of and with the empty time and eventlessness generated by the museum itself and by the programmed cycling of the museum's information panel software. Our work, *The Big Clock*, wanted to just spin there like the revolving racks in the lobby's coat check area and the revolving doors. We came into the museum like bad tourists and we left in the same way.

GUAGNINI: The intersection between power, oppression and sexuality that emerges when Houellebecq describes the social realm in which his narratives take place is what has a Foucaultian dimension for me.

How can you tell a good tourist from a bad one? Or a good artist from a bad one?

KELSEY: A good tourist enters the museum to educate himself or at least to bask in the aura of its treasures, probably reads all the wall texts and rents an audioguide, pays attention. Likewise, a good artist sees the museum as an archive to be studied, mastered and extended. Something like that. A bad tourist only goes to the museum against his better instincts, or goes because there's nowhere else to go, same as he goes to department stores or a Broadway show. A bad artist is a good tourist. A good artist is in his best moments a bad tourist.

GUAGNINI: I don't know what makes you think that between *The Department of Eagles*, new media, and the conceptual art galleries (formerly known as the prints and illustrated books lateral depository) there is not already a guaranteed place for bad boys/good artists/bad tourists/iconoclasts post-flaneurs. We have already been pre-archived, and probably by the curators whom we have been dining with, as MoMA underwent a major generational change. What I learned working on the other side, as you put it, is that all the liberal humanist aspirations of the museum are alive and kicking, both out there factually and within myself. Yes, it's a place where people travel in time, meet eventually, have some kind of experience that Broadway or Yankee Stadium cannot give them (and only for 20 bucks!).

When I was a teen I was kind of nerdish and could only pick up girls in museums or bookstores. The museum is deeply transformative, at least for the co-opted contestatory types like me. I go to museums, any museum, anywhere in the world, and have a good time. Only museums, novels and soccer truly entertain me. Museums do give you something.

KELSEY: The best time I ever had at MoMA was some years ago at an Andreas Gursky exhibition. I had dragged a friend along and he was so bored he decided to do a sort of performance in the museum, announcing to the spectators that he was Andreas Gursky in person, explaining that his mission was to make beautiful pictures of the metropolitan disaster and sell them back to us at a profit, that the practice of photography and all the money he was making supported his cocaine habit, etc. The crowd listened and followed him from image to image until the guards caught on and we were kicked out. I think it's all a question of one's relation to one's own archiving there (how to show up or not in an archive that pretends to already include you). I still like the idea of bad tourism as art, or as an attitude towards the archive. For me, this is exactly what Marcel Broodthaers was doing with his museum signage.

GUAGNINI: Remember Maurizio Cattelan greeting visitors like a giant Picasso puppet? There is an official MoMA version even for the prankster.

All along you have been insisting in those moments in which the airtight continuity between criticality and legitimation has a gap, a kind of "outside" where you try to position yourself. Working in the "9 Screens" project I occupied simultaneously the position of artist, curator, institutional accupuncturist and negotiator. I came out of those waters filled with entropic contradictions, and with the conviction that there are no brotherly Broodthaersian signs really available.

Maybe, in a good week, a meta-structure, and contingent to scale. Downscaling is where it is at to retain a modicum of negation. Orchard, Reena and the Lower East Side were about that, too.

KELSEY: I guess it's always possible to produce a gap between oneself and oneself or between the artist and the so-called author of the work, who are not always the same person. Theodor Adorno had a nice idea about the artist acting as a sort of social agent for the aesthetic subject. It's via the gap between these two that the subject elaborates an objective relation to itself in art. As long as there's this gap, or distance, or non-identity, we can actually go to work on the subject in an objective way, or something. Display is one means of creating this gap. And I think Broodthaers pretty much opened the door for all this. He put institutional discourse on display and made it strange. He was the Musuem director/decorator.

GUAGNINI: Sure ... Adorno ... I've been working on "Nic" a lot. I mean objectively. Regarding display and decor, I've always thought that the critical aspect of Broodthaers work is overly emphasized and how comedic both his mechanisms and critiques are is often overlooked. Humor is my objective.

KELSEY: Know any good jokes?

GUAGNINI: Why was Hitler such a bad artist?

KELSEY: I don't know, why?

GUAGNINI: He didn't know when to stop.

That's an Adornian joke. Your best joke is your title for a Richard Prince catalogue essay: "My other painting is a car." Pretty funny for a WASP. Do you have any serious jokes?

KELSEY: Why is the scarecrow so good at his job?

GUAGNINI: Don't know …

KELSEY: Because he's out standing in his field.

GUAGNINI: A joke in the expanded field, meaning hinging on a gap. My best poem follows that logic: cock tail.

Have you tried your hand at poetry?

KELSEY: Besides the 130 page epic poem with Bernadette Corporation, not so much. Poetry has become an official little business that happens in university departments. Its secret, jealous wish is that it can be out where the art and the money is, but it's lost its connection. BC wanted to steal poetry back from the poets, make a poem without a poet, and make it as good-looking as art.

GUAGNINI: Yes, I saw (or did I read?) the invisible hand in that poem. The ability to consolidate identity, to be a demiurge that represents social aspirations and creates ideological and aesthetic markets has been stripped from poets long ago. Architects occupy that position now. Why do you think Broodthaers opted out of poetry?

KELSEY: I don't think he really stopped. Sinking his published poetry in plaster, where it became forever unreadable, is to me a kind of poetry, too. Then there were his open letters and all the other writing that appeared in exhibitions, his text works, sound pieces and films, etc. I see these as poetic gestures about the outside of poetry, by putting poetry into a new kind of relation with the image and with display. Anyway, only a poet can decide not to write poetry, or activate it as im-potentiality.

GUAGNINI: Broodthaers was schooled in the demise of Surrealism. In replacing poetry for a critical poetics of display he is understanding both the shift towards the audience that the specific public space of the art exhibition implies, and the end of poetry as a representative discipline—by this I mean that in the second half of the Twentieth Century poetry is no longer the major theater of ideas. Also a good way to get rid of all that stiff cult of imagery.

Out of Surrealist methodologies we have *detournement* and Broodthaers. The *détournement* is too Cartesian, too dialectic, and too Hegelian; as both Duchamp and Debord are. Broodthaers's abandonment of poetry, and its realization as im-potentiality, is structured as a joke. He stays clear of the reductive didactic logic associated with institutional critique, which it inherited from the most anal retentive aspects of Minimalism. Broodthaers's humor might be the way out of a current disease: the idea that criticality per se is a higher value. And there is no opposition. If you laugh with or at Broodthaers, you always have to ask yourself why.

KELSEY: I'm interested in what could be called immanent modes of critique, or critique that risks abandoning its proper place in order to assume the creative possibilities of its own practice, to elaborate a more conspiratorial relationship with the object it addresses.

"Where is the critique?" That's a *Texte zur Kunst* type of question that we already see coming from a mile away. The demand is for a criticality that locates itself in a recognizable way and that uses a certain established style of discourse, all the while disavowing both its own aesthetic and its own complicity with power. Critique that disavows its own creativity always betrays a certain resentment toward the creativity of the practices it judges. Its favorite insult is to accuse writers of "belle-lettrism," which only proves its own insecurity in language.

I do agree with Adorno that critique should be heretical, and the best jokes are like that too. Recently I was thinking how important *vaudeville* is for a certain generation of post-60s artists, particularly the Pictures Generation in New York, Dan Graham, Cady Noland, etc. It's interesting how these tendencies gravitated toward low forms of entertainment and comedy: masochistic loser stand-ups, clowns, bad acting, Catskills humor, etc. There is something very profane in these attitudes, and Agamben has a nice way of thinking profanity as a rerouting of sacred contents back into the field of everyday use. To profane is to make useful. It's a kind of heretical redistribution.

The demand for critique, on the other hand, smells of the sacred or of an order where certain things are positioned out of reach. But you can't critique something if you can't touch it. There is no more critique in critique.

GUAGNINI: Agamben's short essay "What is an Apparatus?" has popped up consistently in our dialogue. It's turning out to be an important text for this moment. In general, I relate the profane to Georges Bataille, and in particular with menstrual blood and shit as being the ultimate heterogeneity, and the sovereign. The critique of Christianity still pays off for Agamben and Jean-Luc Nancy. Clownishness, self-deprecatory comedy, scatology … I feel at home. There is also an inherently melancholic aspect to this construct (I'm thinking of Mike Smith, for example). But there is also a latent violence that won't be absorbed in mere critique. By the way, in the opening of "Middle Man," Carol Greene asked me the question apropos my mother-daughter pictures, and in its plainest and most direct formulation, "Where is the critique, Nic?" Where is it, John? Let's be critical. That is: let's mourn. Or else let's swine up.

KELSEY: Somebody asked the same question about BC's *The Complete Poem*, as if you could point your finger at it. But as soon as we recognize critique, we put it over there at a safe distance, and nothing is transformed. Someone organizes a round table or symposium (minus alcohol), and suddenly we think we see it again, right there on the table. You know it's critique when the audience is in their seats and nothing is happening. It's pretty rare that art and politics really cross wires, but these are the moments to look for. They're mutually immune to each other, mutually resentful, two worlds built up around the impossibility of ever touching.

But isn't the swine basically an artist? Maybe you just want to finally be an artist. In Germany they say *maler-schwein*.

GUAGNINI: The demand for critique, and for the political, is born out of the exhaustion of politics in western democracies; which in turn funds art festivals where the art produced in places where politics are not in checkmate, like South America, is hailed as a cure, and generally sanitized and misunderstood. Godard said "all art ends up becoming culture." I see the mutual immune condition you describe as domestication. House artists, house of cultures.

Yes, the swine can only be an artist, and conversely, the artist can only be a swine. It's mostly an ego based activity, despite all efforts against authorship and authority. My swine artist hero is Fassbinder ... But then the cult of Fassbinder is a new melancholy. And I am wary of the swine heroic myths of self-destruction *à la* Kippenberger ... essentially, our everyday life is petit-bourgeois and that's the swine we must construct from.

KELSEY: That was the idea hiding in the *jeune-fille*: to transform the commodified, biopolitically self-managed lifestyle into a war machine.

GUAGNINI: What would be the role of sexuality in that war, and in that machine?

KELSEY: I like the idea of playing roles within sexuality but I don't know if sex itself would need a role. In sex, identity politics never really went away because it never got boring there. It's been thriving there all along, staying healthy by staying sick.

I've heard about the liber-teen scene in Argentina, little kids fucking like mad, what's up with that?

GUAGNINI: Yes, that's right. In sex, differences are both ir-reducible and negotiable. I was a teen in Argentina long ago, and it's been a while since I've had sex with an Argentine teen. Generally there, genitalia is not under a religious spell. In America sexuality is everywhere but in sex. Porn mimics some idea of sexuality, and then sex mimics porn. What I think happens in Argentina is that people begin exploring their sexuality at 14, 15, often with the acquiesence or encouragment of their parents. In Buenos Aires there are temporary lodging places called *Albergue Transitorios* with the sole purpose of fucking. They are all over town, in every price range, and this facilitates one or two hour encounters at any time. In New York the logistics of space and time conjugated with money make it difficult to have casual sex.

KELSEY: Maybe it's when we become indifferent to sex and its imperatives that things can get interesting. Maybe sex doesn't want to work ...

GUAGNINI: Between assigned tasks and indifference there is in sexuality always already a potentiality. I don't think any social change is feasible or complete without changes in both sexual behavior and how it's regulated. Ever since the onset of agricultural societies, when marriage and private property became entwined, sex has been a barometer for all oppression. All the battles between religion and secularism in relationship to gender are at the core of any "us and them" rhetoric. Sex is also the place where economic relationships between first and third world become clear cut (back to Houllebecq!).
It would help if you define the imperatives. Also "sexy" art is always ... sexy, isn't that a contemporary catastrophe?

KELSEY: Imperatives, I mean ... back to Foucault, first the imperative to always talk about it (like now), and then the imperative that life and art have to be throbbing and sexy and connected, which of course means demonstrating this in all kinds of laborious and unsexy ways. Painting always has to "come."

GUAGNINI: Throbbing, sexy and connected is the litany that leads to the ultimate imperative, the orgasm. Ultimately the swine wants to come. To find true love, connecting his balls with his heart and mind in a unified stance, selfhood vibrating in a moment of abolishment of the difference between exchange and use value, being here, now, and forever? Or maybe good sex three times a week?

KELSEY: Isn't there a sort of accountant at work, hiding within your psychedelic swine speak? Sometimes I have the feeling that you are in fact obsessed with exchange value and the cost benefits of swine love. But at the same time you're yearning for a kind of Bataillian communication with the other and a total erosion of boundaries and categories. It might be difficult to resolve this need to calculate and quantify your life with this other, more heretical economic impulse.

GUAGNINI: Yes, you're right on every count. It's fucking hell to live like this. I wish I could be cooler (and by that I mean cold, detached, and seemingly effortless) like you. All I have to say is that if that contradictory attempt to destroy boundaries through quantitative and qualitative classification is my differential "value," or my "content," I give it to the world for free, but people still pay for it!

John, you are a fine analytical mind and can surely self-diagnose. What do you ultimately sell? What's your given?

KELSEY: The last thing we sold was an image of a shadow of a palm tree taken outside the Raleigh Hotel in Miami. I don't think I'm selling myself so much as something generic that I also share with you and so many others. As artists, we are all easily replaceable. Our dealers already know this.

We gave you a bad charcoal portrait of yourself with a yellow painted-in nose and a punctured grommet hole for an eye. In exchange you gave us a small sculpture made from a desktop novelty pendulum and a MoMA security crew work schedule.

There's something funny about a man counting up his attributes, checking his personal wallet as he loses himself in collaborative projects, love, orgasms, etc. Because I guess it's not really *his* orgasm, but he needs to be there in order to lose himself there.

GUAGNINI: The desktop item is called *Newton's Craddle*, and it's a reference to Fassbinder's film *The Third Generation* in which all the petit-bourgeois members of a clandestine revolutionary organization have one of these in their apartments. The schedule is actually for bathroom cleaning. I think that there is no self outside marketing and vice versa. You are in a pseudo Bartlebian position of ontological refusal—gentle refusal, you would prefer not to—but the refusals are within situations you constructed: galleries, discourses, social scenes. I think maybe that is our commonality then, this being there to get lost, this moment of constructing to refuse?

KELSEY: In our case, and in much New York practice, Bartleby is never far from P.T. Barnum, and sometimes the ghost of Jack Smith. Smith's stage was a torn down ceiling, a rubble heap, and the three people that found their way to the Plaster Foundation on a certain midnight were never sure when the show was beginning or ending. Still, it was a show.

I agree that what we're probably both working on, in

different ways, is testing the relationship between constructing and refusing within a hyper-productive non-context we both somehow work on extending, like it or not. It seems more and more pointless to sign our refusals here, but then refusing to sign can just end up functioning as another kind of signature.

ISBN 0-923183-46-2 / 978-0-923183-46-2

Printed in Canada by Westcan.

Art Resources Transfer, Inc. is a nonprofit organization dedicated to establishing a more egalitarian access to the arts through publishing (A.R.T. Press) and the free distribution of contemporary art books to public libraries and schools in under-served communities nationwide (D.U.C. Program).

Between Artists is a series of conversation based books that document different positions and strategies of contemporary, critical visual practice. These conversations provide an opportunity for artists to speak clearly about their practice and give readers a better understanding of the power and relevance of the artists' voice in the discussion of larger social issues.

www.artresourcestransfer.org

Series edited by Alejandro Cesarco
Copyedited by Wendy Tronrud